the story of when I was a flower girl

the invitation:

the date & place:

the wedding party:

the day of the wedding:

Thank Heaven for flower girls

Traditions, Fashions, Flowers & Keepsakes

Arlene Hamilton Stewart

Stewart, Tabori & Chang
NEW YORK

contents

the invitation

being

asked to be a

flower girl

is an honor and

a thrill

After the bride, the flower girl is surely the most admired member of the wedding. Every woman wants her wedding to be perfect, and when you are invited to be the flower girl, it is a great compliment from the bride. You might have mixed feelings: excitement, happiness, pride, maybe a little stage fright. You are about to set off on an adventure, one that will leave you with memories to last a lifetime.

This book will help you each step of the way, telling you everything you need to know about being a flower girl, from how to dress to how to walk down the aisle to how to pose for photographs. And it has special places that you can fill with all your mementos to save forever: the wedding invitation, flowers from your bouquet, a photograph of the wedding party, and the souvenirs from the reception. Enjoy every minute!

what it means

CONGRATULATIONS! You're going to be a flower girl. Before you think about everything that's involved, take a long moment to just feel good. After all, the bride and groom think so highly of you, they want you to be part of their wedding. Be sure to thank them ∼ then tell all your friends.

HOW DID FLOWER GIRLS COME ABOUT? In weddings centuries ago, a girl carrying flowers was thought to bring extra good luck to a marriage. Today some brides have only one flower girl, while others have two, four, or even more.

WHAT SHOULD A FLOWER GIRL DO FIRST? Plan your school and activities schedule: Take care of your other responsibilities, so you can enjoy every thrilling moment of this special experience.

you are an

important

part of the

wedding

will be your

best friends

at the wedding

BESIDES THE FLOWER GIRL, the bride and groom often select other friends and relatives to help them at the wedding. A best man attends the groom and ushers help to seat the guests. A young boy or girl may serve as a ring bearer and carry the rings, usually on a pretty pillow, up to the ceremony.

BRIDESMAIDS ARE SPECIAL to the bride, surrounding her with friendship. The maid of honor (a married woman is called a matron of honor) helps the bride with all the preparations for the wedding. That day, she makes sure the bride looks wonderful, fluffing her veil and smoothing her gown before she walks down the aisle, and she keeps an eye on the rest of the wedding party. She knows who goes where at all times and can offer you a helping hand if you're not sure what to do.

THANK HEAVEN FOR FLOWER GIRLS

wedding manners

A FLOWER GIRL DOES MORE THAN JUST WALK down the aisle. She is invited to parties and showers, and she takes part in the rehearsal the night before the wedding. At the reception, she sits at the bride and groom's table with all the attendants.

- When you are introduced, look at the person's face, smile, and say, "Hello, it's nice to meet you." Shake hands when guests extend theirs.
- At the bridal table, always keep your napkin on your lap. If there is more silverware than you are used to, start with the pieces on the outside. Small forks are for salad, larger ones are for the main course.
- At the reception, if people ask you to dance but you don't want to, simply but sweetly say, "No thank you."

IF YOU AREN'T SURE, remember the Flower Girl's Golden Rule: You won't go wrong if you smile!

the best flower

girls look

happy

all day

in the spotlight

the clothes

the

flower girl's

dress is

always

adorable

*L*UCKY FLOWER GIRLS ~ there are more wonderful outfits for them than anyone except the bride! The dress may be simple or fancy: sheer cottons, shimmering taffetas, glowing satins, lovely laces. Skirts can be long or short, and the bows are big and beautiful.

THOUGH THE BRIDE DECIDES what the flower girl wears, she wants you to look your best and feel comfortable. She may choose a dress that matches the bridesmaids', or she may find a very different one. Whether it's a gown that reaches the floor or a cute mini depends on the time of day and how formal ~ or fancy ~ the wedding will be. The fanciest weddings call for long skirts of dressy fabrics like velvet, while an informal ceremony, perhaps at home or in a garden, would be right for more casual clothes such as petticoats of organdy or simple linen jumpers.

a formal

gown will have

special

fittings

BE PATIENT WHEN SHOPPING for your dress
∼ you may have to try on many before finding the
perfect one. This shopping trip is meant to be fun.
Wear comfortable shoes and your prettiest underwear.

IF THE WEDDING IS VERY FANCY, you, like the bride, might wear a gown made just for you. A dressmaker will take your measurements and create a dress that fits you perfectly, made from fabric the bride selects. Or you could wear a gown that you find in a store, and the store will alter it so that it's exactly right. Since most formal dresses require more than one fitting (a visit with a dressmaker), your patience will have to stretch just a little longer. Of course, once your beautiful gown is home, you'll want to show it to your friends ⌒ but don't let anyone try the dress on until after the wedding has taken place.

more

flower girls

will mean that

much more

fun

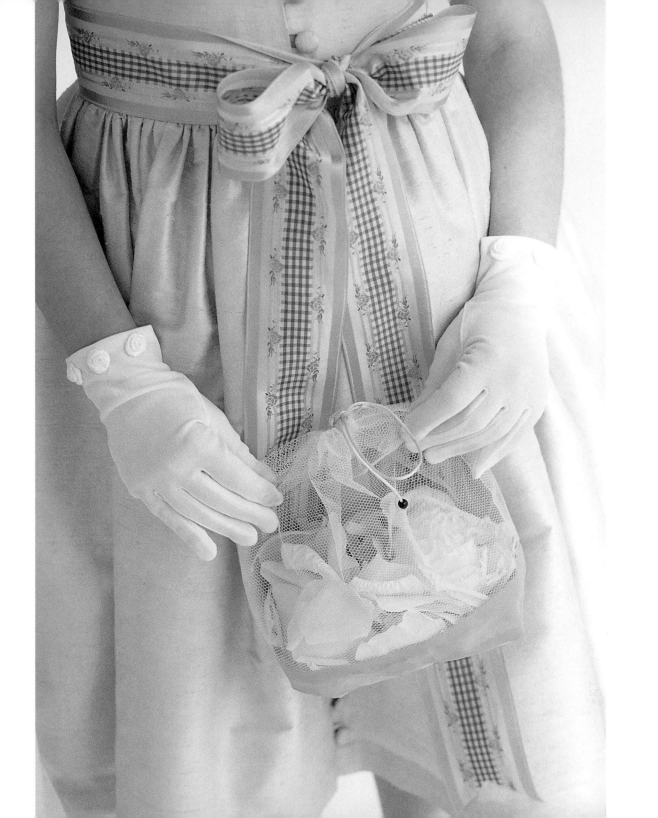

all the extras

FROM HEAD TO TOE, you're going to look fabulous, thanks to the best accessories.

- ❤ JEWELRY Gold lockets on velvet ribbons or necklaces of tiny pearls look lovely. Leave your watch home.
- ❤ HANDBAGS Inside your purse, stash a comb, tissue, lip gloss, a mirror, and a safety pin or two.
- ❤ GLOVES The bride many give you pretty gloves for the ceremony. Take them off at the party afterwards.
- ❤ SHOES You'll wear your shoes ～ ballet slippers, Mary Janes, or pumps ～ for hours. Rough up smooth soles with sandpaper in advance so they won't be slippery.

a private dress

rehearsal

before the

wedding

makes you

comfortable

shiny hair

makes **you** oh

so **pretty**

DRESSING UP LIKE A FAIRY-TALE princess is a thrilling part of being a flower girl. But even Cinderella needed to primp before dazzling everyone at the ball. And so you, too, want to be perfect before sailing down the aisle. That's where extra good grooming comes in. Sparkling hair, teeth, and nails ∽ plus a good night's sleep ∽ are the real flower girl beauty secrets.

♥ HAIR You may wear your hair up in curls or braids, streaming down your back, or all around your face. Whatever style you eventually decide on, a good shampoo is the first step.

♥ TEETH Sometimes flower girls wear braces. Don't worry ∽ you'll look gorgeous with them!

♥ MAKEUP Freshly scrubbed skin is lovely, but a little soft face powder makes your look even prettier in photographs. Check with the bride if you want to wear pale lip gloss or clear nail polish.

♥ PERFUME Ask the bride if you may have a spray of cologne or eau de toilette.

the flowers

bouquets

OURS MAY BE A BOUQUET of sweet garden flowers, such as pansies and violets, tied with satin ribbons, or an old-fashioned nosegay of lilies of the valley from the florist. Perhaps you'll carry just a few perfect roses wrapped in a halo of lace or an armful of French tulips. The tiniest bouquet, known as a tussie-mussie, is often made of fresh herbs like mint and thyme mingled with wild flowers like bluebells and daisies. Long before the wedding day, the bride will have decided on the kind of flowers she wants for everyone, including the groom and his ushers.

AS FLOWER GIRL, your flowers are almost as important as the bride's. They may arrive at home in a tissue-lined box, or at the ceremony ～ or maybe

your most

important

accessory

is also

the prettiest

a flower girl can never have too many flowers

someone will run into the garden minutes before and put together a handful of the bride's favorite blossoms. To carry the bouquet, clasp your hands in front of your waist and hold the flowers by their stems.

baskets

IT HAS LONG BEEN A TRADITION for brides to float down an aisle scattered with flower petals, most often from roses. A long pale piece of fabric covers the length of the aisle, and guests enter from the sides of the room so it stays spotless. First, the other attendants walk down the aisle. Then all heads turn to the entrance ∼ and just moments before the bride, the flower girl appears bearing a basket brimming with petals. Handful by handful, she tosses the petals until she reaches the altar. After the ceremony, the bride takes her new husband's arm and walks back up the petal-strewn aisle, the hems of her gown making the petals flutter. You may walk in front of them, tossing even more petals along the way.

AT SOME WEDDINGS the flower girls hand out rose petals to the guests to toss at the bride and groom instead of rice after the ceremony. Baskets filled with hundreds of loose petals are left at the entrance. Then, as the guests wait outside for the happy couple, the flower girl walks about with the basket on her arm, offering each guest a handful. If you're going to do this, ask the bride to let you practice with the basket before the wedding so that you can get used to handling it.

flowers, like the flower girl, should be treated with great tenderness

hoops & garlands

IMAGINE A BRIGHT, sunny day hundreds of years ago. You've been asked to be a flower girl, along with two or three other young misses. Since there were no florists then, you couldn't expect your bouquet to just show up in a white box on the morning of the wedding. Instead, the bride would count on her bridesmaids to gather flowers and herbs from her garden, which you would wind around hoops and into long garlands.

IF YOU CARRY A HOOP, hold it in one hand, a few inches from the ground. It will take two of you to hold a garland, one from each end. And flower dogs? They get collars of flowers, too!

headpieces

JUST LIKE BRIDES, many flower girls wear headpieces to the wedding. They are a tradition from centuries ago, when newlyweds believed crowns of flowers promised happiness. Flower girls adorn their hair in any number of ways, from very fancy garlands to long, flowing ribbons. Here are the choices:

- A garland encircles your head, and is completely covered with flowers to look as pretty from the back as it does from the front.
- A headband is worn by itself or covered with flowers. It helps keeps hair in place and is perfect for warm summer weddings.
- Ribbons and bows make pretty tie-backs for long hair, and bows of satin, taffeta, or lace look sweet on short hair.

YOU'LL WEAR YOUR HEADPIECE with confidence if you practice a bit first. Small combs and hairpins will hold garlands; barrettes make sure ribbons and bows stay put.

fresh flowers

smell wonderful

and look

pretty

the big day

dressing up

everything

feels so

exciting

you can't

wait to begin

*D*ID WE MENTION HOW IMPORTANT a good night's sleep is? Of course, as the wedding approaches, everyone is excited and maybe a little jittery. You'll find that after the rehearsal, the wedding planned for so long suddenly starts to become very real.

MAKE SURE YOU HAVE PLENTY OF TIME to get ready. Fancy dresses often have a lot of buttons and bows and underskirts to be fastened and arranged. If you have flowers in your hair or are wearing a headdress, take a slow twirl around the room to see if everything stays in place. Speak up if something doesn't feel comfortable. Ask the maid of honor to check that your slip isn't showing and that your bows are fluffed. Take one final look in a full-length mirror to prove what everyone's been saying ～ you are the very best flower girl your bride could ever hope for!

the ceremony

YOU'RE OFF! The bride may be nervous ⌁ she might love it if you planted a little kiss on her cheek or squeezed her hand in yours. And a couple of sure-fire jokes wouldn't hurt.

YOU MAY BE IN A LIMOUSINE, a carriage, a taxi, or on foot. Everyone is so excited ⌁ smoothing their gowns and fussing with their bouquets. Soon, music fills the air, and one by one the bridesmaids proceed down the aisle. Now it's your turn. (Traditionally, the flower girl walks right in front of the bride, but if there are two or more of you, you may walk down the aisle before the bridesmaids.) A deep breath, a quick wink to the bride, and out you go.

WALK SLOWLY. If you feel scared, look at something right in front of you. When you get to the end of the aisle, turn around and watch the bride wearing your happiest smile.

the bride

will want

you to be

near her

catching sight of

the flower **girl**

sends a murmur of

delight through

the guests

the best flower girl is pretty, poised, and, well, perfect

the party

FLASH BULBS POP AND ROSE PETALS fly through the air. The bride rides with her new husband, and you'll travel to the party in the car with the bridesmaids. There you might join the newlyweds' families and the attendants in the receiving line, so that you can say hello to all the guests.

FIND YOUR PLACE AT THE TABLE, and if you're tired of carrying your flowers, tuck them under your seat. At most weddings, a toast to the bride and groom is made before the meal. You'll be served juice or soda. Stand with everyone, raise your glass, and take a sip when the toast is completed.

AS PART OF THE FLOWER GIRL'S DUTIES, you could be asked to hand out small wedding presents to the guests. You may notice that everyone is especially happy and lively, and many people will make a big fuss over you. That's your reward for being adorable!

the flower girl is noticed by everyone, so keep smiling

THANK HEAVEN FOR FLOWER GIRLS

you may **want** to

jump for **joy** or

collapse in

your **chair**

FINALLY, WEDDING JITTERS GIVE WAY TO FUN. The families of the newlyweds say hello to each other; relatives who have not seen each other in a while are reunited; stories are told and songs are sung. When the meal is finished, the bride and groom will join hands to cut their beautiful wedding cake together.

THE DAY IS going by so quickly. Your final performance: After a first twirl with his bride, the groom may ask you for a dance. If you feel nervous, practice a moment in a corner before taking center stage.

hold that pose

photographers

capture

all the best

moments

THOUGH IT ALL SEEMS TO BE ENDING too fast, there will be photographs and videotapes that have recorded the day. The bride may talk with you before the wedding about photographs, both posed portraits and candid shots. There will be several portraits of the entire wedding party, then some of you alone with the bride. Guests often bring cameras, and they'll want photos of you, too. Check in a mirror before the photographer begins, and, as your mother has always told you, stand up straight. Try to let your face reflect the happiness you feel.

FLOWER GIRLS CAN ALSO bring their own cameras to the wedding. A wonderful gift for the bride and groom would be an album of pictures taken at the wedding by their very own flower girl, put together with other mementos of the celebration.

Other members
of the **bridal**
party hold the
flower girl in
great esteem

good-bye

THE DEPARTURE OF THE NEWLYWEDS signals that the celebration is winding down. Guests share a last dance, then bid good-bye to you and the couple's parents. After the months of planning and practice and fantasizing, the wedding is over, and it has been as wonderful as your every dream. Write down your feelings now, while they are fresh, on the memento pocket at the back of this book. Tuck flowers, ribbons, and photographs into the book's tulle sleeves.

A FLOWER GIRL NEVER really says good-bye. The bride and groom will cherish your "gifts" ⟳ your sweet smile, your graceful performance. Long after the guests have forgotten the meal or the music, they will remember the flower girl with soft smiles and maybe a quiet chuckle. And you, most of all, will keep within your heart the joy and love you shared this day.

your day is

done, and you will

always keep

these memories

© 1999 Smallwood & Stewart, Inc.

Published in 1999 by
Stewart, Tabori & Chang
A division of U.S. Media Holdings, Inc.
115 West 18th Street
New York, NY 10011

Distributed in Canada by
General Publishing Company Ltd.
30 Lesmill Road
Don Mills, Ontario, Canada M3B 2T6

Library of Congress Cataloging in Publication Data is available upon request.

Printed in Singapore

10 9 8 7 6 5 4 3 2 1

ISBN 1-55670-869-6

Library of Congress Catalog Card Number: 98-88350

To place an order, please call (800) 932-0070
or fax (800) 732-8688
To inquire about publicity, please call (212) 519-1262
or fax (212) 519-1210

Designed by Debbie Sfetsios

Produced by Smallwood & Stewart, Inc.
New York City

Photography Credits:

Mary Adele
32, 38

Joshua Ets-Hokin/Ets-Hokin Studios
8, 34 bottom right, 35, 39 top left, 39 top right, 43

Oberto Gili
front and back cover, 47

Joyce Heisen/Casual Candids
27 top, 44-45

Thomas Hooper, Victoria Magazine
18

Phil Kramer
10, 11, 16, 17, 19, 20, 29, 31, 33, 34 top, 34 bottom left, 37, 40 top, 41

Elyse Lewin, Victoria Magazine
4-5

Toshi Otsuki, Victoria Magazine
7, 21, 22, 24, 28, 39 bottom

Michael Skott, Victoria Magazine
15

Linda Slocum
25

Carlos Spaventa, Victoria Magazine
42

William Stites
26, 27 bottom, 40 bottom

Stuart-Rogers Ltd.
12